Chapter 1 Introduction

The web application contemporary has really come a long way over the years with the introduction of many popular frameworks such as bootstrap, angular JS, etc. All these frameworks are based on the JavaScript framework popular.

But when it was to develop applications based on server, there was a kind of empty, and it is there that node.js is entered in the image.

Node.js is also based on the JavaScript framework, but it is used for the development of applications based on server. While browsing the whole of the tutorial, we will examine node.js in detail and how we can use it to develop applications based on server.

WHAT IS NODE.JS?

Node.js is a runtime environment for open-source and cross platform used for the development of server-side Web applications. The applications node.js are written in

JavaScript and can be executed on a wide variety of operating systems.

Node.js is based on an event architecture and an API of input/output, non-blocking designed to optimize throughput and scalability of an application for web applications in real time.

Over a long period of time, the available framework for Web development was based on a model without state. A model without state is a model in which the data generated in a session (such that the information on the user settings and the events that have products) are not managed to be used in the next session with this user.

A lot of work had to be done to maintain the information of session between the requests of a user. But with node.js, finally there is a way for web applications to have a bidirectional connection in real time, where the client and the Server can initiate communication, which enables them to exchange data freely.

WHY USE NODE.JS

We will examine the real value of node.js in the forthcoming chapters, but what is it that makes this framework if famous. Over the years, most of the requests were based on a framework of response to requests without state. In this type of applications, it is up to the developer to ensure that the correct code has been put in place to ensure that the status of the Web session has been maintained while the user was working with the system.

But with the Web applications node.js, you can now work in real time and have a bi-directional communication. The state is maintained and the client or the server can start the communication.

CHARACTERISTICS OF NODE.JS

Let us look at some of the main characteristics of node.js.

1.   The asynchronous I/O controlled by event helps to the simultaneous processing of queries - it is probably the biggest argument of sale of node.js. This characteristic essentially means that if a request is received by node for an input/output operation, it will execute the operation in

the background and will continue to deal with other applications.

It is very different from the other programming languages. A simple example of this is given in the code below

```
VAR FS = REQUIRE('FS');



FS.READFILE("SAMPLE.TXT",FUNCTION(ERROR,DATA)


    {
                CONSOLE.LOG("READING                    DATA
COMPLETED");
});
```

- The code snippet above focuses on the playback of a file called sample.txt. In other programming languages, the line of treatment following just would take place that once the whole file is read.

- But in the case of node.js the significant fraction of the code to be noted is the declaration of the function ('function(error,data)'). This is what is called a callback function.

- As well, what is happening here is that the operation of reading of the file will start in the background. And Other treatments may take place simultaneously during the reading of the file. Once the reading operation of the file is complete, this anonymous function will be called and the text "Reading data completed" will be written in the log of the console.

2. Node uses the execution engine JavaScript v8, the one that is used by Google Chrome. Node has a wrapper on the JavaScript engine that makes the execution engine much faster and therefore the processing of queries in node also becomes more rapid.

3. Treatment of concurrent queries - Another key feature of node is the possibility of dealing with concurrent connections with a minimum of overhead costs on a single process.

4.   The library node.js has used JavaScript - this is another important aspect of the development of node.js. A large part of the community of development are already well paid in javascript, and therefore, the development in node.js becomes more easy for a developer who knows javascript.

5.   There is a vibrant and active community for the framework node.js. Because of the active community, there are always updates to Key put at the disposal of the Framework. This allows to keep the Framework is always up to date with the latest trends in the Web development.

Who uses node.js?

Node.js is used by a variety of large companies. You will find below a list of a few of them.

•   Paypal - many sites within Paypal have also begun the transition on node.js.

- LinkedIn - LinkedIn uses node.js to power its mobile servers, which feed the products iPhone, Android and Mobile Web.

- Mozilla has implemented node.js to withstand the API of browser that has a half-billion of facilities.

- Ebay hosts its HTTP service API in node.js.

WHEN TO USE AND DO NOT USE NODE.JS

Node.js is the best for use in streaming or in applications in real time based on events such as

1. Applications of chat rooms

2. The game servers - servers fast and effective who need to deal with thousands of requests to the times, then it is an ideal framework.

3. Good for the collaborative environment - it is good for environments that manage the documents. In the Management Environment of documents, you will have several people who displayed their documents and make constant changes in checking and verifying the documents. Therefore node.js is good for these environments because

the loop of events in node.js can be triggered each time that documents are modified in a management environment of documents.

4.   Servers advertising - Here again, you might have thousands of applications to remove advertisements of the central server and node.js can be an ideal framework to manage this.

5.   Streaming Servers - another ideal scenario to use node is for the streaming servers multimedia where customers have queries for extract different multimedia content of this server.

Node.js is good when you need high levels of concomitance but less CPU time dedicated.

Best of all, because node.js is built on javascript, c is the best suited when you build client-side applications that are based on the same javascript framework.

When not to use node.js

Node.js can be used for a large number of applications for various purposes, the only scenario where it should not be used is if there is long periods of treatment that is required by the application.

The node is structured to be simple thread. If an application is necessary to perform long calculations in the background. Therefore, if the server made calculations, it will not be able to treat other queries. As indicated above, node.js is the best solution when the treatment requires less CPU time dedicated.

Chapter 2: Download and install node.js

To begin to build your applications node.js, The first step is the installation of the framework node.js. The framework node.js is available for a variety of operating systems, from Windows to Ubuntu and OS X. Once the framework node.js is installed, you can begin to build your first applications node.js.

Node.js also has the possibility to integrate external features or extended features using custom modules. These modules must be installed separately. An example of a module is the module MongoDB that allows you to work with databases MongoDB from your application node.js.

HOW TO INSTALL NODE.JS

The first step in the use of node.js is the installation of the Libraries node.js on the client system. To perform the installation of Node.js, follow the steps below;

Step 1) go on the site Https://nodejs.org/en/download/ and download the binary files needed. In our example, we will download the installation files 32-bit for node.js.

Step 2) Double-click the file.msi downloaded to start the installation. Click the Run button in the first screen to begin the installation.

Step 3) In the next screen, click on the "Next" button to continue the installation.

Step 4) In the following screen accept the license agreement and click on the Next button.

Step 5) In the next screen, choose the location where node.js must be installed, and then click the Next button.

1.   First enter the location of the file for the installation of Node.js. It is here that the files of node.js will be stored after the installation.
2.   Click on the Next button to continue the installation.

Step 6) accept the components by default and click the Next button.

Step 7) In the next screen, click the Install button to start the installation.

Step 8) Click on the Finish button to complete the installation.

INSTALLATION OF A NODE THROUGH THE INTERMEDIARY OF A MANAGER OF PACKETS

The other way to install node.js on any client machine is to use a "manager of packets".

On Windows, the manager of packets of nodes is known under the name of chocolatey. It was designed to be a decentralized framework to quickly install the applications and tools that you need.

To install node.js via Chocolatey, the following steps must be carried out.

Step 1) Installation of Chocolatey - The Web site of Chocolatey (Https://chocolatey.org/) contains very clear instructions on how this framework must be installed.

• The first step is to execute the command below in the windows of the command prompt. This command is extracted from the web site of Chocolatey and is the standard command for the installation of Node.js via chocolatey.

• The command below is a PowerShell command that calls the script remote PowerShell on the site chocolatey. This command must be executed in a command window PowerShell.

• This script PowerShell does all the necessary work to download the necessary components and install accordingly .

@Powershell -NoProfile -ExecutionPolicy Bypass -command "iex will ((new-object wet.webclient).DownloadString('Https://chocolatey.org/install.ps1'))" && SET PATH=%PATH%;%ALLUSERSPROFILE%\chocolatey\bin

Step 2) The next step is to install node.js on your local machine using the package manager chocolatey. This can be done by running the following command in the command prompt.

Cinst nodejs install

If the installation is successful, you will get the message of the successful installation of Node.js.

Note: If you get an error such as "C:\ProgramData\chocolatey\lib\libreoffice\tools\chocola teyInstall.ps1" and then manually delete the folder in the path.

RUN YOUR FIRST HELLO WORLD APPLICATION IN NODE.JS

Once you have downloaded and installed node.js on your computer, try to display "Hello World" in a web browser. Create the file node.js with the file name firstprogram.js

```
Var http = require('HTTP');

Http.createServer(function (req, Res) {
    Res.writeHead(200, {'Content-Type': 'text/html'});
```

```
Res.end('Hello World!');
}).Listen(8080);
```

Code Explanation:

1. The basic functionality of the "require" function is that it reads a JavaScript file, runs the file, then returns an object. Has the help of this object, then you can use the different features available in the module called by the required function. Therefore in our case, since we want to use the functionality of HTTP and we use the command require(http).

2. In this 2nd line of code, we create a server application that is based on a simple function. This function is called each time that a request is made to our server application.

3. When a request is received, we ask our function to return a response "Hello World" to the customer. The writeHead function is used to send data from header to the client and

while the final function will close the connection to the client.

4. We use then the function .Listen to ensure that our application server listens for client requests on port 8080. You can specify any available port here.

Run the code

Step 1) Save the file on your computer: C:\Users\Your Name\Your Name\premierprogramme.js

Step 2) In the command prompt, navigate to the folder in which the file is stored. Enter the command

Firstprogram node.js

Step 3) Now, your computer operates as a server! If someone tries to access your computer on port 8080, he will get a "Hello World! Return message!

Step 4) Start your Internet browser and type in the address: http://localhost:8080

OutPut

Summary

• We have seen the installation of Node.js via the module of MSI installation which is available on the web site of node.js. This installation installs the necessary modules to the execution of an application node.js on the client.

• Node.js may also be installed via a package manager. The Package Manager for Windows is known under the name of chocolatey. By running simple commands in the command prompt, the manager of packets Chocolatey automatically downloads the necessary files and installs on the client machine.

• A simple application node.js is to create a server that listens on a particular port. When a request arrives on the server, the client automatically sends a reply Hello World' to the customer.

Chapter 3: Modules

A module in node.js is a logical encapsulation of code in a single unit. It is always a good programming practice to always separate the code so that it is easier to manage and maintain for purposes in the future. It is here that the modules of node.js come into action.

As each module is an independent entity with its own encapsulated functionality, it can be managed as a unit of work separately.

During this tutorial, we will see how we can use the modules in node.js.

WHAT ARE THE MODULES IN NODE.JS?

As indicated previously, the modules in Node js are a way to encapsulate the code in a unit separate logic. There are many modules ready to employment on the market that can be used in Node JS.

Here are a few of the popular modules that are used in an application node JS.

1. Express framework - Express is a web application framework node minimum JS and hose that provides a robust set of features for the web and mobile applications.

2. Socket.io - Socket.IO allows a event communication real-time two-way. This module is good for the creation of applications based on the cat.

3. Jade - Jade is a template engine high performance and implemented with JavaScript for the nodes and the browsers.

4. MongoDB - The driver MongoDB node.js is the driver node.js officially supported for MongoDB.

5. Restify - restify is a lightweight framework, similar to express for the construction of REST API.

6. Bluebird - Bluebird is a library of promises complete with an emphasis on the innovative features and performance.

USE OF MODULES IN NODE.JS

In order to use the modules in an application node.js, they must first be installed using the package manager node. The command line below shows how a module of "express" can be installed.

Npm install Express

- The above command will download the necessary files which contain the "Modules Express" and will also the installation.
- Once the module is installed, to use a module in an application node.js, you must use the keyword'require'. This keyword is a means that node.js uses to incorporate the functionality of a module in an application.

Let us look at an example of the use of the keyword "require". The example of code "Guru99" below shows how to use the function required.

VAR EXPRESS=REQUIRE(EXPRESS');

```
VAR APP=EXPRESS();
APP.SET('VIEW EMNGINE','JADE');
APP.GET('/',FUNCTION(REQ,RES)
{
});
VAR SERVER=APP.LISTEN(3000,FUNCTION()
{
});
```

1.   In the first declaration itself, we use the keyword "require" to include the module Express. The module "express" is a JavaScript library optimized for the development of node.js. It is one of the modules node.js most commonly used.

2.   Once the module is included, in order to use the features of the module, an object must be created. Here, a module object Express is created.

3.   Once the module is included using the command "require" and that a "object" is created, the required methods of the module Express can be invoked. Here, we use the set command to set the engine of view, which is used to define the template engine used in node.js. Note:- (just for the understanding of the reader, a template engine is an approach to inject values in an application by collecting data from data files. This concept is quite famous in angular JS where the curly braces fastened {{{Key}} are used to substitute values in the web page. The word key' in the curly braces fastened refers essentially to the variable that will be replaced by a value when the display of the page.

4.   Here, we use the method of listening to listen to the application on a particular port number.

CREATION OF MODULES NPM

Node.js has the possibility to create custom modules and allows you to include these custom modules in your application node.js.

Let us look at a simple example of the way in which we can create our own module and include this module in our main application file. Our module will only a simple task to add 2 numbers.

Follow the steps below to see how we can create modules and include them in our application.

Step 1) Create a file called "Addition.js" and include the code below. This file will contain the logic of your module.

Below is the code that would be in this file;

```
Var exports=module.exports={};
Exports.AddNumber=function(a,b)
{
Return a+b;
};
```

1.   The keyword "exports" is used to ensure that the functionality defined in this file is actually accessible by other files.

2.   We are in the process of defining a function called AddNumber The'. This function is defined to take 2 parameters, a and b. The function is added to the module "exports" to make the function a public service accessible by other modules of application.

3.   We are finally making of our function return the value added of the settings.

Now that we have created our custom module which has the functionality to add 2 numbers. It is now time to create an application, who will call this module.

In the next step, we will see how to create the application that will call our custom module.

Step 2) Create a file called "APP.js", which is your main application file and add the following code

```
Var addition=require('./Addition.js');
Console.log(addition.AddNumber(1.2));
```

1.   We use the keyword "require" to include the functionality in the file addition.js.

2.   Since the functions of the file addition.js are now accessible, we can now make a call to the function AddNumber. In the function, we spend 2 numbers as parameters. We have then the value in the console.

Output:

•   When you run the file app.js, you will get a value output 3 in the console log.

•   The result is that the function AddNumber in the file addition.js was called with success and that the returned value of 3 has been displayed in the console.

Note: - We do not use yet the "Node package manager" to install our module addition.js. In effect, the module is already part of our project on the local machine. The package manager NODE originates in the image when you publish a module on the Internet that we see in the next topic.

EXTENSION MODULES

During the creation of modules, it is also possible to extend or inherit a module from another module.

In the modern programming, it is quite common to build a library of common modules and extend the functionality of these common modules if necessary.

Let us look at an example of the way in which we can extend the modules in node.js.

Step 1) Create the base module.

In our example, create a file called "Tutorial.js" and place the code below.

In this code, we are in the process of creating a function that returns a string of characters to the console. The string returned is "Guru99 Tutorial".

```
VAR EXPORTS=MODULE.EXPORTS={};
EXPORTS.TUTORIAL=FUNCTION()
{
CONSOLE.LOG("GURU99 TUTOTIAL")
}
```

1.   The export module is used so that any function defined in this file may be available in other modules of node.js.

2.   We are in the process of creating a function called tutorial which can be used in other modules node.js.

3.   We display a string of characters "Guru99 Tutorial" in the console when this function is called.

Now that we have created our basic module called the Tutorial.js. It is now time to create another module which will extend this basic module.

We will examine how to achieve it on to the next step.

Step 2) Next, we will create our module extended. Create a new file called "NodeTutorial.js" and place the code below in the file.

Var Tutor=require('./Tutorial.js');

Exports.NodeTutorial=function()

```
{
Console.log("Node Tutorial")
Function pTutor()
{
Var PTutor=Tutor
PTutor.tutorial;
}
}
```

Note the following key points about the code above

1.   We use the "require" function in the new file from the module itself. Since we are going to extend the file to existing module "Tutorial.js", we must first the include before of the extend.

2.   We then create a function called "Nodetutorial". This function will do 2 things,

•   It will send a string of characters "Node Tutorial" to the console.

- It will send the string "Guru99 Tutorial" the basic module "Tutorial.js" to our extended module "NodeTutorial.js".

1. Here, we conduct the first step to send a string of characters to "Node Tutorial" to the console.
2. The next step is to call the function from our module Tutorial, which will remove the string "Guru99 Tutorial" toward the console.log.

Step 3) Create your file app.js principal who is your main application file and include the code below.

Var localTutor=require('./NodeTutorial.js');
LocalTutor.NodeTutorial();
LocalTutor.NodeTutorial.pTutor();

The code above is the following things;

1.   Our main application file is now called the module "NodeTutorial".

2.   We call the function "NodeTutorial". In calling this function, the text "Node Tutorial" will be displayed in the console log.

3.   Since we have extended our module Tutorial.js and exposed a function called pTutor. It also calls the module tutorial in the module Tutorial.js, and the text "Guru99 Tutorial" will also be displayed on the console.

Output:

Since we have implemented the Code app.js above by using node, we get the following output in the console file.log.

- Tutorial on the nodes
- Guru99 tutorial of Guru99

Publication of the modules NPM(Node Package Manager) Modules

It may publish its own module in its own Filing Github.

By publishing your module to a central location, you do not have to install on all machines that are in need.

Instead, you can use the installation command of NPM and install your module NPM published.

The following steps must be followed to publish your module NPM

Step 1) create your repository on GitHub (a tool for the management of repository of code in line). It can be used to host your deposits of code.

Step 2) You need to tell your local installation NPM who you are. This means that we must say to NPM who is the author of this module, what is the email ID and any URL of company available which must be associated with this identifier. All these details will be added to your module NPM when it will be published.

The commands below define the name, the e-mail address and the URL of the author of the NPM module.

Npm init.author.name set "Guru99".

Npm set init.author.author.email "Guru99@gmail.com"

Npm set init.author.url http://Guru99.com

Step 3) The next step is to connect to NPM using the identification information provided during the last step. To connect, you must use the command below

Npm login

Step 4) Initialize your package - the next step is to initialize the package to create the file package.Json. This can be done by issuing the command below

Npm init

When you run the command above, you will be prompted to reply to certain questions. The most important is the version number of your module.

Step 5) Publish on GitHub - The next step is to publish your source files on Github. This can be done by running the commands below.

Git add.

Git commit -m "Initial Release"

Git tag v0.0.1

Push git Origin master --tags

Step 6) Publish your module - The last bit is to publish your module in the Registry NPM. This is done via the command below.

Npm Publish

MANAGEMENT OF THIRD PARTY PACKAGES WITH NPM

As we have seen, the "Node package manager" has the capacity to manage the modules, which are required by the Applications node.js.

Let us look at some of the functions available in the package manager of nodes for the management of the modules.

1.   Install the packages in Global mode - The modules can be installed at the global level, which simply means that these modules would be available for all projects node.js on a local machine.

The example below shows how to install the "Module Express" with the Global option.

Npm install express -Global

The Global option in the above statement is what allows you to install the modules at a global level.

2.   List of all packages installed overall on a local machine. This can be done by running the following command in the command prompt

Npm list --global

Below is the output that will be displayed if you have already installed the "Module Express" on your system.

Here you can see the different modules installed on the local machine.

3.   Install a specific version of a package - sometimes it may be necessary to install only the specific version of a package. Once you know what is the package and the relevant version that should be installed, you can use the command to install NPM to install this version specific.

The example below shows how to install the module called underscore with a specific version of 1.7.0.

Npm install underscore@1.7.0

4.   Updating a version of Packet - Sometimes, you can have an old version of a package in a system, and you can want to update to the latest version available on the market. To do this, we can use the command NPM update.

The example below shows how to update the package underscore to the latest version.

Npm update underscore

5.   Search for a particular package - to search for if a particular version is available on the local system or not, you can use the command to search for NPM. The example below will verify if the module Express is installed on the local machine or not.

Npm search Express

6.   Uninstall a package - the same thing in which you can install a package, you can also uninstall a package. The uninstalling a package is done with the uninstall command of NPM.

The example below shows how to uninstall the module Express.

Npm uninstall Express

WHAT IS THE FILE PACKAGE.JSON?

The file "package.Json" is used to contain the metadata of a particular project. This information provides the manager of packets of the crossroads the information necessary to understand how the project should be treated with its dependencies.

The package files.Json contain information such as the description of the project, the version of the project in a particular distribution, the license information and the configuration data.

The file package.JSON is normally located at the root of a project node.js.

Let us take an example of the structure of a module when it is installed via the NPM.

The snapshot below shows the contents of the file of the module Express when it is included in your project node.js. From the Snapshot, you can see the file package.JSON in the folder Express.

If you open the file package.JSON, you will see a lot of information in the file.

Below is a snapshot of a part of the file. The Express@~4.13.1 mentions the version number of the module express used.

Summary

• A module in node.js is a logical encapsulation of code in a single unit. The separation in modules makes the code easier to manage and maintain for purposes in the future.

• There are many modules available on the market that can be used in node.js such as express, underscore, mongoDB, etc.

• The package manager of nodes (NPM) is used to download and install the modules which can then be used in an application node.js.

• You can create modules custom NPM, extend these modules and publish these modules.

- The package manager node has a complete set of commands to manage the NPM modules on the local system such as the installation, the uninstall process, research, etc.

- The file package.JSON is used to contain all of the metadata of a NPM module.

Chapter 4: Create a server and obtain data

The framework node.js is mainly used to create applications based on server. The framework can easily be used to create web servers that can be used for content for users.

There are a variety of modules such as the modules "http" and "request", which help to treat requests related to the server in the Server space Web. We will see how we can create a core application of Web server using node JS.

NODE AS A WEB SERVER USING HTTP

Let us look at an example of how to create and run our first Application Node JS.

Our application will create a simple server module which will listen on port no. 7000. If a request is made by the intermediary of the browser on this port No., the application server will send a reply Hello' World' to the customer.

```
Http var=require('HTTP')
Var server=http.createServer((function(request,response)
{
    Response.writeHead(200,
    {"Content-Type": "text/plain"));
    Response.end("Hello World\n");
}));
Server.listen(7000);
```

Code Explanation:

1.   The basic functionality of the function of requirement is that it reads a javascript file, runs the file, and then proceeded to return the object of export. As well, in our

case, since we want to use the functionality of the HTTP module, we use the function require to obtain the required functions from the HTTP module so that it can be used in our application.

2.	In this line of code, we create a server application that is based on a simple function. This function is called each time that a request is made to our server application.

3.	When a request is received, we ask you to send a response with a header of type '200'. This number is the normal response that is sent in an HTTP header when a successful response is sent to the customer.

4.	In the response itself, we send the string Hello World'.

5.	We use then the function server.Listen to ensure that our application server listens for client requests on port no. 7000. You can specify any available port here.

If the command is executed successfully, the following output is displayed when you run your code in the browser.

Output:

From the output,

- You can clearly see that if we navigate toward the URL of localhost on port 7000, you will see the string Hello World', as displayed in the page.

- Because in our code we mentioned specifically for the server to listen on the port no. 7000, we are able to see the result when navigating to this URL.

Here is the code of your reference

```
Http var=require('HTTP')

Var server=http.createServer((function(request,response)

{

Response.writeHead(200,

{"Content-Type": "text/plain"));

Response.end("Hello World\n");
```

```
}));
```

```
Server.listen(7000);
```

TREATMENT OF GET REQUESTS IN NODE.JS

Make a GET request to obtain the data to another site is relatively simple in node.js. To make a GET request in the node, we must first have the request module installed. This can be done by running the following line in the command line

Npm install request

The above command request to the manager of packets node to download modules of required query and install accordingly. When your NPM module has been successfully installed, the command line will display the name and the version of the installed module: <name>@<version>.

In the snapshot above, you can see that the module'request' with the version number 2.67.0 has been downloaded and installed.

Let us now look at the code that can use this command'request'.

```
Var request = require("Request");

Request("Http://www.google.com",function(error,respons
e,body)
    {
        Console.log(body);
    });
```

Code Explanation:

1.   We use the module'require' which has been installed at the last step. This module has the necessary functions which can be used to perform GET requests to Web sites.

2.   We are doing a GET request to www.google.com and then call a function when a response is received. When a response is received, the parameters (error, response and body) will have the following values

•   Error - In case of error received when the use of the GET request, it will be registered here.

•   Answer- The answer will be the HTTP headers that are returned in the response.

•   Body- The body will contain the full content of the reply sent by Google.

•   In this case, we write simply the received content in the body parameter in the file console.log. So, basically, everything that we will get by going to www.google.com will be written on the console.log.

Here is the code of your reference

```
Var request = require("Request");

Request("Http://www.google.com",function(error,respons
e,body)

{

Console.log(body);

});
```

Summary

•	The framework node.js can be used to develop web servers by using the module http'. The application can be made to listen on a particular port and send a reply to the customer each time a request is made to the application.

•	The module'drequest' can be used to obtain information from Web sites. The information would contain the entire contents of the requested web page to the Web site concerned.

Chapter 5: node.js with Express

In this tutorial, we will also examine the framework Express. This framework is built in such a way that it acts as a framework for web application node.js minimal and flexible, providing a robust set of features for the construction of a simple web application and multipage, and a web application hybrid.

WHAT IS EXPRESS.JS?

Express.js is a node js web application server framework, which is specifically designed for the construction of web applications one pager, multi-page and hybrid.

It has become the framework of standard server for node.js. Express is the rear part of something known under the name of stack mean.

The mean is a software stack free JavaScript and open-source for the creation of dynamic Web sites and Web applications whose components are the following;

1) MongoDB - The standard database NoSQL

2) Express.js - The framework by default web applications

3) Angular.js - The JavaScript Framework MVC Used for web applications.

4) node.js - Framework used for scalable applications on the server side and network.

The framework Express.js makes it very easy for the development of an application that can be used to address multiple types of requests such as queries GET, PUT, POST, and DELETE.

INSTALLATION AND USE OF EXPRESS

Express Installs via The Package Manager node. This can be done by running the following line in the command line

Npm install Express

The above command request to the manager of packets node to download modules express required and install accordingly.

Use our new framework Express and create a simple "Hello World" application.

Our application will create a simple server module which will listen on port no. 3000. In our example, if a request is made via the browser on this port No., then the application server will send a reply Hello' World' to the customer.

```
Var express=require( Express');
Var app=express();
App.get('/',function(req,res)
{
    Res.send('Hello World!');
});


Var server=app.listen(3000,function() {});
```

Code Explanation:

1.	In our first line of code, we use the function require to include the module Express.

2.	Before you can begin to use the module Express, we must make a module object Express.

3.	We create here a callback function. This function will be called each time that someone will sail up to the root of our web application that is http://localhost:3000 . . The callback function will be used to send the string Hello World' to the web page.

4.	In the callback function, we refer the string "Hello World" to the customer. The parameter'res' is used to return the content to the web page. This parameter'res' is something that is provided by the module'request' to allow to send content to the web page.

5.	We use then the function Listen to to ensure that our application server listens for client requests on port no. 3000. You can specify any port available here.3

If the command is executed successfully, the following output is displayed when you run your code in the browser.

Output:

From the output,

• You can clearly see that if we navigate toward the URL of localhost on port 3000, you will see the string Hello World', as displayed in the page.

• Because in our code we mentioned specifically for the server to listen on the port no. 3000, we are able to see the output when navigating to this URL.

WHAT ARE THE ROUTES

The routing is used to determine how the application responds to a request from a customer to a final point particular.

For example, a customer can do a query GET, POST, PUT, PUT or delete http for various URL like the one shown below;

Http://localhost:3000/Books

Http://localhost:3000/Students

In the example above,

- If a GET request is made for the first URL, then the answer should ideally be a list of books.
- If the GET request is made for the second URL, then the answer should ideally be a list of students.
- Thus, on the basis of the URL which is accessed, a different functionality on the web server will be invoked and, accordingly, the response will be sent to the customer. It is the concept of routing.

Each route can have one or several management functions, which are performed during the mapping of the road.

The general syntax of a route is the following

App.method(path, Handler)

Where

1) APP is an instance of the module Express

2) method is a method of HTTP request (GET, POST, PUT, PUT or delete).

3) path is a path on the server.

4) handler is the function to be performed when the pairing of the route.

Let us look at an example of the way in which we can implement itineraries in Express. Our example will create 3 routes as follows

1.   A road /node that will display the string "Tutorial on Node" if it accesses to this route.

2.   A road /block which will display the string "Tutorial on angular" if it accesses to this route.

3.   A default route / who will display the string "Welcome to Guru99 Tutorials".

Our code base will remain the same as the previous examples. The EXTRACT Below is an add-on to show how the routing is implemented.

```
App.Route('/node).get(function(req.res)
{
Res.send("tutorial on Node");
```

```
});
App.Route('/angular).get(function(req.res)
{
Res.send("tutorial on angular");
});
App.get('/',function(req,res)
{
Res.send('Welcome to Guru99 Tutorials');
});
```

Code Explanation:

1. Here, we define a route if the URL http://localhost:3000/Node is selected in the browser. We attach to the route a callback function that will be called when we will sail toward the URL of the node.

The function has 2 parameters.

• The main parameter that we will use is the parameter'res' which can be used to return information to the client.

• The parameter'req' contains information on the current request. Sometimes, additional parameters may be sent in the framework of the application, and therefore the parameter'req' can be used to find the additional parameters sent.

2. We use the Send function to return the string "Tutorial on Node" to the customer if the route node is chosen.

3. Here, we define a route if the URL http://localhost:3000/Angular is selected in the browser. Has the route, we attach a callback function that will be called when we will sail toward the URL angular.

4. We use the Send function to return the string "Tutorial on angular" to the customer if the road angular is chosen.

5. It is the default route that is chosen when it navigates to the route of the application -http://localhost:3000. When the default route is chosen, the message "Welcome to Guru99 Tutorials" will be sent to the customer.

If the command is executed successfully, the following output is displayed when you run your code in the browser. Output:

From the output,

• You can clearly see that if we navigate toward the URL of localhost on port 3000, you will see the string a Welcome to Guru99 Tutorials' displayed on the page.

• Because in our code, we mentioned that our default URL would show this message.

From the output,

• You can see that if the URL has been changed in /node, the route of the respective node would be chosen and the string "Tutorial on Node" is displayed.

From the output,

- You can see that if the URL has been changed in /angular, the route of the respective node would be chosen and the chain of characters "Tutorial on angular" is displayed.

EXAMPLE OF WEB SERVER USING EXPRESS.JS

From our example above, we have seen how we can decide which output display depending on the routing. This type of routing is what is used in most of the modern Web applications. The other part of a web server with the use of models in Node JS.

During the rapid creation of applications node on the fly, a quick and simple way is the use of models for the application. There are many executives available on the market for the creation of models. In our case, we will take the example of the framework of jade for the template.

Jade Installs via The Package Manager node. This can be done by running the following line in the command line

Npm install jade

The above command request to the manager of packets node to download modules required jade and install accordingly.

Use our framework newly Jade installed and create a few basic models.

Step 1) The first step is to create a model in Jade. Create a file called index.jade and insert the following code

1.   Here we specify that the title of the page will be changed to any value that is passed when this template is invoked.

2.   We also specify that the text in the tag header will be replaced by what is spent in the template jade.

Var express=require(Express');

Var app=express();

```
App.set('View engine','Jade');

App.get('/',function(req,res)

{

    Res.render( Index',

        {Title:'Guru99',Message:'Welcome'})

});

Var server=app.listen(3000,function() {});
```

Code Explanation:

1.   The first thing to specify in the application is "Engine of view" which will be used for the rendering of the models. Since we are going to use jade to make our models, we specify in consequence.

2. The function of rendering is used to make a Web page. In our example, we make the model (index.jade) which was created earlier.

3. We turn the values of "Guru99" and "Welcome" to the settings "title" and "message" respectively. These values will be replaced by the parameters'Title', and'message' declared in the model index.jade.

If the command is executed successfully, the following output is displayed when you run your code in the browser.

Output:

From the output,

• We can see that the title of the page is set to "Guru99" and that the header of the page is set to "welcome".

• It is because of the template jade which is invoked in our application js node.

Summary

• The framework Express is the framework most commonly used for the development of the Applications node JS. The framework Express is built on the framework node.js and allows you to accelerate the development of applications based on server.

• The roads are used to divert users to different parts of the web applications in function of the request made. The answer for each route can vary depending on what must be shown to the user.

• The models can be used to inject the content in an effective manner. Jade is one of the engines of template The most popular and used in the Applications node.js.

Chapter 6: node.js with MongoDB

Most of the modern Web applications have a kind of system of data storage to the background to store the data. For example, if you take the case of an application to purchase online, data such as the price of an article or the number of items of a particular type would be stored in the database.

The framework Node js has the ability to work with databases which are commonly required by the most modern web applications. Node js can also operate well with relational databases (such as Oracle and MS SQL

Server) that with non-relational databases (such as MongoDB and MySQL). During this tutorial, we will see how we can use the databases from the Applications node JS.

THE DATABASES NODE.JS AND NOSQL

Over the years, the NoSQL databases such as MongoDB and MySQL are become very popular as databases for the storage of data. The ability of these databases to store any type of content and in particular in any format is what makes these databases if famous.

Node.js has the capacity to work with MySQL and MongoDB as databases. To use the one or the other of these databases, you must download and use the required modules using the package manager node.

For MySQL, the required module is called "mysql" and for the use of MongoDB, the module to install is "Mongoose".

With these modules, you can perform the following operations in node.js

1. Manage the pool of connections - it is here that you can specify the number of connections to the MySQL database which must be maintained and backed up by node.js.

2. Create and close a connection to a database. In both cases, you can provide a callback function that can be called each time that the methods of connection "create" and "close" are executed.

3. The requests can be executed to obtain data of the respective databases in order to retrieve the data.

4. These modules also allow you to perform data manipulation such as inserting, deleting and updating of the data.

For the other topics, we will see how we can work with databases MongoDB in node.js.

USE OF MONGODB AND NODE.JS

As we have seen above, MongoDB is one of the databases the most popular used with node.js.

In the course of this chapter, we will see

How to establish connections with a database MongoDB

How can we carry out the normal operations of reading data from a database as well as the insertion, deletion and update records in a database MongoDB.

For the purposes of this chapter, let us assume that the data MongoDB below are in place.

The name of the database: EmployeeDB

Name of the collection: Employee

Documents

```
{
    {Employeeid: 1, Employee Name: Guru99},
    {Employeeid: 2, Employee Name: JOE},
    {Employeeid: 3, Employee Name: Martin},
}
```

1.   Installation of the NPM modules to access Mongo from an application node, a driver is necessary. There are a number of drivers Mongo available, but MongoDB is among

the most popular. To install the module MongoDB, run the following command

Npm install mongodb

2. Create and close a connection to a database MongoDB. The code snippet below shows how to create and close a connection to a database MongoDB.

```
Var MongoClient = require('mongodb').MongoClient;
Var url = 'Mongodb://localhost/EmployeeDB';

MongoClient.connect(url, function(err, db) {

    Cursor.log("connected");

    Db.close();

});
```

Code Explanation:

1.   The first step is to include the module mongoose which is done through the function require. Once the module in place, we can use the necessary functions available in this module to create connections to the database.

2.   Then, we specify our chain of connection to the database. In the connection string, there are 3 key values which are transmitted.

•   The first is'mongodb' which specifies that we connect to a database MongoDB.

•   The following is'localhost', which means that we connect to a database on the local machine.

•   The following is the EmployeeDB' which is the name of the database defined in our database MongoDB.

3.   The next step is to connect to our database. The function of connection takes into account our URL and has the ability to specify a callback function. It will be called when the connection to the database will be open. This

gives us the opportunity to know if the connection to the database has been successful or not.

4.   In the function, we write the string "connection" on the console to indicate that a successful connection has been created.

5.   Finally, we close the connection using the instruction db.Close.

If the above code is executed correctly, the string "connected" will be written to the console as shown below.

3.   Search for data in a database MongoDB - Using the driver MongoDB, we can also retrieve data from the database MongoDB.

The section below will show how we can use the driver to retrieve all the documents from our collection of employees (it is the collection of our database MongoDB which contains all the documents relating to employees. Each document has an object ID, the name of the employee and the Employee ID to define the values of the document) in our database EmployeeDB.

```
Var MongoClient = require('mongodb').MongoClient;
Var url = 'Mongodb://localhost/EmployeeDB';

MongoClient.connect(url, function(err, db) {

  Var Cursor = db.collection('employee').find();

  Cursor.chaque(function(err, doc) {

    Console.log(DOC);

  });
});
```

Code Explanation:

1.   In the first step, we create a cursor (A cursor is a pointer that is used to point to the different records retrieved from a database. The cursor is then used to iterate

through the different records in the database. Here, we define a variable name called cursor that will be used to store the pointer to the records retrieved in the database. Pointing to the records retrieved in the collection MongoDb. We also have the possibility to specify the collection "Employee" from which to retrieve the records. The FIND function() is used to specify that we want to retrieve all the documents of the collection MongoDB.

2.   We are in the process of iterate through our cursor and for each document in the Cursor, we are going to execute a function.

3.   Our function is simply to print the content of each document on the console.

Note: - It is also possible to retrieve a particular record from a database. This can be done by specifying the search condition in the find function(). For example, suppose that if you want to simply retrieve the registration of which the name of the employee is Guru99, then this statement can be written   as   follows: "var cursor=db.collection('employee').find()".

If the above code is executed with success, the following output will be displayed in your console.

Output:

From the output,

- You can clearly see that all documents in the collection are retrieved. This is possible by using the Find() method of the connection MongoDB (DB) and iterating all documents using the cursor.

4.   Insertion of documents in a collection - The documents can be inserted in a collection using the method insertOne provided by the Library MongoDB. The code snippet below shows how to insert a document in a collection MongoDB.

```
Var MongoClient = require('mongodb').MongoClient;
Var url = 'Mongodb://localhost/EmployeeDB';

MongoClient.connect(url, function(err, db) {
```

```
Db.collection('employee').insertOne({
    The employeeid: 4,
    EmployeeName: "NewEmployee"
  });
});
```

Code Explanation of the Code:

1.   Here, we use the method insertOne of the Library MongoDB to insert a document in the collection of the employees.

2.   We specify the details of the document of which must be inserted in the collection of the employees.

If you now check the contents of your database MongoDB, you will find the registration with the employeeid 4 and EmployeeName of "NewEmployee" inserted in the collection employee.

Note: The console will not display any output because the record is inserted in the database and that no output can be displayed here.

To verify that the data have been inserted correctly in the database, you must run the following commands in MongoDB

1.   Use EmployeeDB
2.   Db.Employee.find({Employeeid :4 })

The first Declaration guarantees that you are connected to the database EmployeeDb. The second statement is seeking the registration of which the identification number of the employee is 4.

5.   Update of documents in a collection - Documents may be updated in a collection using the method updateOne provided by the Library MongoDB. The code snippet below shows how to update a document in a collection MongoDB.

```
Var MongoClient = require('mongodb').MongoClient;
Var url = 'Mongodb://localhost/EmployeeDB';


MongoClient.connect(url, function(err, db) {
```

```
Db.collection('employee').updateOne({

    "EmployeeName": "NewEmployee"

}, {

    $SET: {

        "EmployeeName": "Mohan"

    }

});

});
```

Code Explanation:

1.   Here, we use the method "updateOne" of the Library MongoDB, which is used to update a document in a collection MongoDB.

2.   We specify the search criteria of the document to update. In our case, we want to find the document that has the name of the employee to "NewEmployee".

3.   Then we want to set the value of the name of the employee of the document of "NewEmployee" to "Mohan".

If you now check the contents of your database MongoDB, you will find the registration with the employeeid 4 and EmployeeName of "Mohan" updated in the collection employee.

To verify that the data have been properly updated in the database, you must run the following commands in MongoDB

1.   Use EmployeeDB

2.   Db.Employee.find({Employeeid :4 })

The first Declaration guarantees that you are connected to the database EmployeeDb. The second statement is seeking the registration of which the identification number of the employee is 4.

6.   Deletion of documents in a collection - Documents can be deleted in a collection using the method "deleteOne" provided by the Library MongoDB. The code snippet below shows how to delete a document of a collection MongoDB.

Var MongoClient = require('mongodb').MongoClient;

```
Var url = 'Mongodb://localhost/EmployeeDB';

MongoClient.connect(url, function(err, db) {

   Db.collection('employee').deleteOne(

      {
         "EmployeeName": "Mohan"
      }

   );
});
```

Code Explanation:

1.   We use here the method "deleteOne" of the Library MongoDB, which allows you to delete a document of a collection MongoDB.

2.   We specify the search criteria in the document to delete. In our case, we want to find the document that has

the name of the employee to "Mohan" and delete this document.

If you now check the contents of your database MongoDB, you will find the registration with the employeeid 4 and EmployeeName of "Mohan" removed from the collection employee.

To verify that the data have been properly updated in the database, you must run the following commands in MongoDB

1. Use EmployeeDB

2. Db.Employee.find()

The first Declaration guarantees that you are connected to the database EmployeeDb. The second reading research and displays all the records in the collection of the employees. Here you can see if the record has been deleted or not.

HOW TO BUILD AN APPLICATION NODE EXPRESS WITH MONGODB TO STORE AND SERVE THE CONTENT.

Build an Application with a combination of the two in using Express and MongoDB is very common to our days.

When working with web applications based on JavaScript, we will speak normally here of the term mean stack.

• The term mean stack refers to a collection of technologies based on JavaScript used to develop web applications.

• MEAN is the acronym of MongoDB, ExpressJS, AngularJS and node.js.

It is therefore always good to understand how node.js and MongoDB work together to provide applications that interact with databases backbones.

Let us look at a simple example of the way in which we can use "express" and "MongoDB" together. Our example will use the same collection of employees in the database MongoDB EmployeeDB.

We will now incorporate Express to display the data on our web page when they are requested by the user. When our application is running on node.js, it may be that the need to navigate to the URL http://localhost:3000/Employeeid.

When the page is launched, all identification numbers of employees of the collection of employees will be displayed. So let us look at the code snippet in the sections that will enable us to achieve it.

Step 1) define all of the libraries that must be used in our application, which in our case is both the library MongoDB and the Library Express.

Code Explanation:

1. We are in the process of defining our library Express', which will be used in our application.

2. We are in the process of defining our library Express', which will be used in our application to connect to our database MongoDB.

3. Here, we define the URL of our database to which to connect.

4.   Finally, we are in the process of defining a string of characters that will be used to store our collection of identifiers of employees who will be displayed in the browser by the suite.

Step 2) In this step, we will now get all the documents of our collection "employees" and work with them accordingly.

Code Explanation:

1.   We are in the process of creating a route to our application called the employeeid'. As well, each time that someone browses http://localhost:3000/Employeeid of our application, the extract of code defined for this route will be executed.

2.   Here, we get all of the records in our collection'employee' through the command db.collection('employee').find(). We then assign this collection to a variable called a cursor. In using this variable

of the cursor, we will be able to browse through all of the records in the collection.

3.   We now use the function cursor.Each() to navigate through all of the records in our collection. For each record, we will define a snippet of code on what must be done when access to each record.

4.   Finally, we see that if the recording returned is not null, then we take the employee via the command "item.Employeeid". The rest of the Code is that to build a appropriate HTML code that will allow our results to be displayed   correctly   in   the   browser.

Step 3) In this step, we will send our output on the web page and do listen to our application on a particular port.

Code Explanation:

1.   Here we send the entire content which has been built in the previous step to our Web page. The parameter'res' allows us to send content to our web page in response.

2. We ensure that any our application node.js listening on port 3000.

Output:

From the output,

• It shows clearly that all parts of the identity of the employees of the collection of the employees have been recovered. It is because we use the driver MongoDB for us to connect to the database and retrieve all records of employees and then used "Express" to display the records.

Here is the code of your reference

```
Var Express = require( Express');
Var App = express();
Var MongoClient = require('mongodb').MongoClient;
Var url = 'Mongodb://localhost/EmployeeDB';
Var str = "";


App.Route('/Employeeid').get(function(req, res)
```

```
{
    MongoClient.connect(url, function(err, db) {
        Var Cursor = db.collection('employee').find();
        //Noinspection JSDeprecatedSymbols
        Cursor.chaque(function(err, item) {

            If (item != null) {
                Str = str + "Employee ID " + item.Employeeid + "";
            }
        });
        Res.send(str);
        Db.close();
    });
});


Var server = app.listen(3000, function() {});
```

Note:cursor.Each can be depreciated according to the version of your driver MongoDB. You can add

//noinspection JSDeprecatedSymbols before cursor.Each to circumvent the problem. Alternatively, you can use a foreach loop. Below is the code for the example of use foreach.

```
Var Express = require( Express');
Var App = express();
Var MongoClient = require('mongodb').MongoClient;
Var url = 'Mongodb://localhost/EmployeeDB';
Var str = "";


App.Route('/Employeeid').get(function(req, Res) {
  MongoClient.connect(url, function(err, db) {
    Var collection = db.collection('employee');
    Cursor var = collection.find({});
    Str = "";
    Cursor.ForEach(function(item) {
      If (item != null) {
          Str = str + "Employee ID " + item.Employeeid + "";
      }
```

```
  }, Function(err) {
     Res.send(str);
     Db.close();

   }
  );
 });
});
Var server = app.listen(8080, function() {});
```

Summary

• Node.js is used in conjunction with the NoSQL databases to build a large number of modern Web applications. Some of the common databases used are MySQL and MongoDB.

• One of the common modules used for working with databases MongoDB is a module called'MongoDB'. This module is installed via the package manager node.

• With the module MongoDB, it is possible to query the records of a collection and to perform the normal operations of update, deletion and insertion.

- Finally, one of the modern practices is to use the framework express with MongoDB to deliver modern applications. The framework Express can use the data returned by the pilot MongoDB and display the data to the user in the Web page accordingly.

Chapter 7: Promise, generator, event and FILESTREAM

In the previous tutorials, you would have seen the callback functions which are used for the asynchronous events. But sometimes the callback functions can become a nightmare when they begin to nest, and the program begins to become long and complex.

In such cases, node.js provides additional functionality to correct the problems encountered during the use of the callbacks. These are classified in Promises, generates and events. During this tutorial, we will learn and see these concepts in more detail.

WHAT ARE THE PROMISES

Before you begin with promises, first, let's review what are the functions of "Callback" in node.js. We have seen many things these callback functions in the previous chapters, then let us move quickly to review one of them.

The example below shows a snippet of code, which is used to connect to a database MongoDB and perform an update operation on one of the records in the database.

1.   In the code above, the part of the public(err,db) is known under the name of declaration of an anonymous function or reminder. When the MongoClient creates a connection to the database MongoDB, it returns to the callback function once the connection operation is complete. Therefore, in a sense, the operations of connection are in the background, and when it is done, he calls our callback function. Remember that it is one of the key points of node.js to allow many operations to occur simultaneously and do not prevent a user to perform an operation.

2. The second block of code is what is executed when the callback function is actually called. The callback function does that update a record in our database MongoDB.

Then, what is a promise? Well, a promise is that an improvement of the callback functions in node.js. During the course of the development cycle, there may be an instance where you need to nest several callback functions together. This can become a kind of disorder and difficult to maintain at a certain moment in time. In short, a promise is a improvement of reminders to the work which aims to mitigate these problems.

The basic syntax of a promise is shown below;

```
VAR BRIDE = DOSOMETHINGAYNC()
BRIDE.THEN(ONFULFILLED, ONREJECTED)
```

- "DoSomethingAync" is a callback function or asynchronous which is a kind of treatment.

- This time, when the definition of recall, there is a value that is returned called "promise".

- When a promise is returned, it can have 2 outputs. This is defined by the "clause of the time". Either the operation can be a success, which is indicated by the parameter onFulfilled The'. Or he can have an error which is denoted by the parameter onRejected The'.

Note: The key aspect of a promise is therefore the return value. There is no concept of return value when working with reminders normal in node.js. Because of the return value, we have more control over the way in which the callback function can be defined.

In the next topic, we will see an example of promises and how they benefit the reminders.

REMINDERS TO PROMISES

Now let us look at an example of how we can use the "Brides" from an application node.js. In order to use promised in an application node.js, the module the promise' must first be downloaded and installed.

We will change then our code as shown below, which updates an Employee name in the collection employee' using promises.

Step 1) Installation of Modules NPM

To use brides from a Node application JS, the Promised module is necessary. To install the module Promise, run the command below

Npm install Bride

Step 2) modify the code to include the promises.

```
Var Bride = require('promise');
Var MongoClient = require('mongodb').MongoClient;
Var url = 'Mongodb://localhost/EmployeeDB';

MongoClient.connect(url)
```

```
.Then(function(err, db) {
  Db.collection('employee').updateOne({
    "EmployeeName": "Martin"
  }, {
    $SET: {
      "EmployeeName": "Mohan"
    }
  });
});
```

Code Explanation:-

1.   The first part is to include the module the promise'
which will allow us to use the functionality of promise in
our code.

2.   We can now add the functionaln'then' to our function
MongoClient.connect. As well, when the connection to the
database is established, we must run the extract of code
defined by the suite.

3.   Finally, we define our extract of code that does the work to update EmployeeName of the employee with the name of "Martin" to "Mohan".

Note: -

If you now check the contents of your database MongoDB, you will find that if a record with the name of the employee "Martin" exists, it will be updated in "Mohan".

To verify that the data have been inserted correctly in the database, you must run the following commands in MongoDB

1.   Use EmployeeDB

2.   Db.Employee.find({EmployeeName :Mohan })

The first Declaration guarantees that you are connected to the database EmployeeDb. The second search the registration which bears the name of the employee "Mohan".

TREAT THE NESTED PROMISES

When the definition of promises, it should be noted that the method "at the time" returns itself a promise. Thus, in a sense, the promises can be nested or chained to each other.

In the example below, we use the Web to define 2 callback functions, which all insert two a record in the database MongoDB.

(Note: The chaining is a concept used to bind the execution of methods to each other. Let us assume that your application has 2 methods called'methodA' and'methodB'. And the logic was such that'methodB' should be called after'methodA', then you enchaîneriez the execution so that'methodB' is called directly after'methodA').

The key thing to note in this example is that the code becomes more clean, readable and maintainable using promises nested.

Var Bride = require('promise');
Var MongoClient = require('mongodb').MongoClient;
Var url = 'Mongodb://localhost/EmployeeDB';

```
MongoClient.connect(url)

.Then(function(db) {
    Db.collection('employee').insertOne({
        The employeeid: 4,
        EmployeeName: "NewEmployee"
    })

    .Then(function(db1) {
        Db1.collection('employee').insertOne({
            The employeeid: 5,
            EmployeeName: "NewEmployee1"
        })
    })
});
```

Code Explanation:-

1.   We are in the process of defining 2 Clauses 'to the time" that are executed one after the other. In the first

clause, we turn the parameter'db' which contains our connection to the database. We use then the property of collection of the connection'dB' to insert records in the collection Employees'. The method the insertOne' is used to insert the real document in the collection of the employees.

2.   We use then the clause 2nd then to insert another record in the database.

If you now check the contents of your database MongoDB, you will find the 2 records inserted in the database MongoDB.

GENERATE PROMISES WITH THE BLUEBIRD LIBRARY

Bluebird is a library full promise for JavaScript. The characteristic the strongest Bluebird is that it allows you to "promise" other modules node in order to use asynchronously. Promisify is a concept applied to callback functions. This concept is used to ensure that each callback function that is called returns a sort of value.

Thus, if a module node js contains a callback function that does not return a value, if we promise the module node, all the functions of this module of the specific node would automatically be modified to ensure that it returns a value.

You can therefore use BlueBird to operate the module MongoDB asynchronously. This fact only add another level of ease during the writing of the Applications node.js.

We will look at an example of the use of the module Bluebird.

Our example will first establish a connection with the "Employee collection" in the database "EmployeeDB". If the connection "then" is established, it will obtain all the documents in the collection and will display in the console accordingly.

Step 1) Installation of Modules NPM

To use Bluebird from an application node, the module Bluebird is necessary. To install the module Bluebird, run the command below

Npm install bluebird

Step 2) The next step is to include the Bluebird module in your code and to promise the module MongoDB in full. By promise, we intend that bluebird will ensure that each method defined in the library MongoDB returns a promise.

Code Explanation of the code:-

1.   The command require is used to include the library Bluebird.

2.   Use the method .promiseifyAll() from Bluebird To create an asynchronous version of all the methods provided by the module MongoDB. This ensures that each method of the module MongoDB runs in the background and that a promise is returned for each method call in the library MongoDB.

Step 3) The final step is to connect to our database, retrieve all records of our collection and display them in our console log.

Code Explanation of the code:-

1. You will notice that we use the method "connectAsync" instead of the method of normal connection to connect to the database. Bluebird adds in fact the keyword Async for each method of the Library MongoDB to distinguish the calls that return of the promises and those who do not. There is therefore no guarantee that the methods without the word Async will return a value.

2. As for the method connectAsync, we now use the findAsync method to return all of the records in the collection'employee' of MongoDB.

3. Finally, if findAsync returns a Successful promise, we define then a block of code to iterate through each record in the collection and display in the console log.

If the above steps are executed properly, all the documents in the collection of the employees will be displayed in the console as shown in the output below.

Here is the code of your reference

Var Bride = require('Bluebird');

```
Var                mongoClient                =
Promise.promisifyAll(require('mongodb')).MongoClient;

Var url = 'Mongodb://localhost/EmployeeDB';
MongoClient.connectAsync('mongodb://localhost/Employe
eDB')

.Then(function(db) {
    Return db.collection('employee').findAsync({})

})
.Then(function(cursor) {
  Cursor.chaque(function(err, doc) {
    Console.log(DOC);
  })
});
```

CREATE A CUSTOM PROMISE

A custom promise can be created using a module of node called'Q'. The Library'q' must be downloaded and installed using the package manager of node. After having used the library'q', the method "denodeify" can be called, which fact that any function becomes a function that returns a promise.

In the example below, we will create a simple function called "Add" which will add 2 numbers. We are going to convert this function in a function to return promise.

Once this is done, we will use the promise returned by the Add function to display a message in the console file.log.

Follow the steps below to create our custom function to return a promise.

Step 1) Installation of Modules NPM

To use'q' from a Node application JS, the module'q' is necessary. To install the module'q', run the command below

Npm install q

Step 2) define the following code code that will be used to create the custom promise.

Var Q= require('Q');

```
Function Add() {
    Var a, b, c;
    A=5;b=6;
    C=A+B;

}
```

Var Display_bride= Q.denodeify(Add);

Promised var=Add;

Bride.Then
{Console.log("addition function complete");}

Code Explanation of the code:-

1.   The first bit is to include the library'q' using the keyword required. Using this library, we can define any function to return a reminder.

2.   We are in the process of creating a function called Add that will add 2 numbers defined in the variables a and b. The sum of these values will be stored in the variable C.

3.   We then use the library Q for dénodifier (the method used to convert any function in a function that would return a promise) Our function add or to convert our function Add to a function that returns a promise.

4.   We now call our function "Add" and are able to obtain a value of promise to return due to the previous step that we have carried out of dénodifier The Add function.

5.   The keyword to then' is used to specify that if the function is executed with success, then displays the string "Addition function completed" in the console file.log.

When the above code is executed, the output "Function of addition complete" will be displayed in the console.log file as shown below.

THAT ARE THE GENERATORS

The generators are become quite famous in node.js these last time and this probably because of what they are able to do.

- The generators are of the executions of the functions that can be suspended and times later.

- The generators are useful when it is run of concepts such as the execution lazy. This essentially means that by suspending the execution and resuming at will, we cannot draw the values that when we need it.

The generators were the 2 methods The following keys

1. Method of performance - the method of performance is called in a function to stop the execution of the function to the specific line where the method of performance is called.

2. Following method - This method is called from the main application to resume the execution of a function which has a method of performance. The execution of the

function will continue until the next method of performance or until the end of the method.

Let us look at an example of the way in which the generators can be used.
In our example, we are going to have a simple add function which will add 2 numbers, but we will continue to stop the execution of the method at different points to show how the generators can be used.

```
Function* Add(x) {
   Yield x + 1;
   Var y = yield(null);
   Y = 6
   Return x + y;
}

Var gen = add(5);
```

```
Gen.next();

Gen.next();
```

Code Explanation of the code:-

1. The first step is to define the "function" of our generator. Note that this is done by adding a "*" to the keyword of the function. Then we are in the process of defining a function called Add that takes a parameter of x.

2. The keyword yield is a specific keyword to the generators. This makes it a powerful construct to pause a function in the middle of anything. Thus here, the execution of the function will be stopped until we are invoking the following function(), which will be done in step 4. At this point, the value of x will become 6 and the execution of the function will be stopped.

3. It is here that we call the function first generator and send the value of 5 to our function Add. This value will be substituted in the x parameter of our function Add.

4. Once that we call the function next(), the function Add() will resume the execution. When the next instruction var y= yield(null) will be executed, the function Add() stop again the execution.

5. Now, after having called the function again next(), the next instructions will be executed, and the combined value of x=6 and y=6 will be added and returned.

REMINDERS VS. THE GENERATORS

The generators are used to solve the problem of what is called the hell of the reminder. Sometimes, the callback functions become so intertwined during the development of an application node.js that it becomes too complicated to use the callback functions.

It is here that the generators are useful. One of the most common examples is the creation of the timer functions.

See the example below which shows how the generators can be useful in relation to the reminders.

Our example will only create a simple timer function. We would like to then call this function incorporating a delay of 1000, 2000 and 3000 ms.

Step 1) define our callback function with the code of the delay required.

Code Explanation of the code:-

1.	Here we create a function called Timedelay with a parameter called ptime. This will take the necessary time that we want to introduce in our application.

2.	The next step is simply to create a message that will be displayed to the user saying that the application will be paused during these few milliseconds.

Step 2) Let us now look at the code if we incorporate the reminders. Suppose that we want to incorporate reminders based on the value of 1000, 2000 and 3000 milliseconds, the code below shows how we should implement them using the Reminders.

Code Explanation:-

1.   We call the timedelay as a callback with 1000 as value.

2.   Then, we want to call the function again Timedelay with 2000 as the value.

3.   Finally, we want to call the function again Timedelay with 3000 as the value.

From the above code, you can see that it becomes more disorderly because we want to begin to call the function several times.

Step 3) Let us now see how to implement the same code using generators. From the code below, you can now see at what point it became easy to implement function Timedelay using generators.

Code Explanation of the code:-

1.   We are in the process of defining a function of generator that will be used to call our Timedelay function.

2. We call the function yield with the timedelay function with 1000 as the parameter value.

3. Then we call the YIELD function and the function Timedelay with 2000 as the value of parameter.

4. Finally, we call the function yield with the timedelay function with 3000 as the value of parameter.

THE FILESTREAM IN NODE.JS

Node makes heavy use of flows as a mechanism for the transfer of data.

For example, when you pull out something to the console using the function Console.log, you use in fact a stream to send the data to the console.

Node.js also has the ability to stream the data in the files so that they can be read and written in an appropriate manner. We will now consider an example of the way in which we can use the stream to read and write from files. For this example, we must follow the following steps

Step 1) Create a file called data.txt file that contains the data below. Let us assume that this file can be stored on the drive of our local machine.

Tutorial on node.js

Introduction

Events

The generators

Data connectivity

Use of the Jasmin

Step 2) Write the relevant code which will use the stream to read the data from the file.

```
Var fs = require("FS");
Var stream;
Stream = fs.createReadStream("D://data.txt");

Stream.On("data", function(data) {
    Var chunk = Data.toString();
    Console.log(chunk);
```

```
});
```

Code Explanation of the code:-

1.   First we need to include the Modules The fs' which contain all the features necessary to the creation of flow.

2.   Then we create a readable flow using the method - createReadStream. In entry, we indicate the location of our file data.txt.

3.   The steam function.There is a manager of events and in the latter, we specify the first parameter as'data'. This means that each time that data arrives in the stream from the file, then run a callback function. In our case, we are in the process of defining a callback function that will run 2 basic steps. The first is to convert the data read from the file in the form of a string of characters. The second would be to send the string of characters converted to output to the console.

4.   We take each piece of data that is read from the data stream and the convert to a string of characters.

5. Finally, we send the output of each piece of rope converted to the console.

Output:

• If the code is executed correctly, you will see the output above in the console. This output will be the same as that of the file data.txt.

Write to a file

In the same way that we create a stream of reading, we can also create a stream to write to write data in a file. First create an empty file without content called data.txt. Let us assume that this file is placed in the drive of our computer. The code below shows how we can write data to the file.

```
Var fs = require("FS");
Var stream;
Stream = fs.createWriteStream("D://data.txt");

Stream.write("tutorial on node.js")
```

```
Stream.write("Introduction")

Stream.write("Events")

Stream.write("generators")

Stream.write("Data Connectivity")

Stream.write("Using Jasmine")
```

Code Explanation of the code:-

1.   We create a writable stream using the method createWriteStream. In entry, we indicate the location of our file data.txt.

2.   Then, we have used the method stream.Write to write the different lines of text in our text file. The flow will write these data in the file data.txt.

If you open the file data.txt, you will now see the following data in the file

Tutorial on node.js

Introduction

Events

The generators

Data connectivity

Use of the Jasmin

PIPES IN NODE.JS

In the Applications node, the flows can be channelled together using the pipe method(), which takes two arguments:

• A flow of required writing which serves as the destination for the data and the data.

• An Optional object used to pass in the options.

A typical example of the use of pipes, if you want to transfer data from a file to the other.

So let us look at an example of the way in which we can transfer data from a file to the other with the help of pipes.

Step 1) Create a file called datainput.txt file that contains the data below. Let us assume that this file can be stored on the drive of our local machine.

Tutorial on node.js

Introduction

Events

The generators

Data connectivity

Use of the Jasmin

Step 2) Create a file empty empty called dataOutput.TXT and place it on the D drive of your local machine.

Step 3) Write the code below to perform the data transfer of the file datainput.txt to the file dataOutput.txt.

Code Explanation of the code:-

1.   We first create a "readstream" toward our datainput file.txt which contains all our data which must be transferred to the new file.

2.   We must then create a "writestream" toward our dataOutput file.txt, which is our empty file and which is the destination for the transfer of the file data datainput.txt.

3. We then use the command pipe for transfer the data playback stream to the flow of writing. The control pipe will take all the data that arrive in the readstream, and will push toward the flow of writing.

If you now open the file dataOutput.txt, you will see all the data present in the file datainput.txt.

EVENTS IN NODE.JS

The events are one of the key concepts of node.js and sometimes node.js is designated under the name of event framework.

Basically, an event is something that occurs. For example, if a connection is established to a database, the event of connection to the database is triggered. The Event-Driven Programming is to create functions that will be triggered when specific events are triggered.

Let us look at a basic example of definition of an event in node.js.

We will create an event called 'data_received'. When this event is triggered, the text "Data received" will be sent to the console.

```
Var events = require( Events');
Var eventEmitter = new events.EventEmitter();
EventEmitter.It('data_received', function() {
    Console.log('Data received succesfully.');
});


EventEmitter.emit('data_received');
```

Code Explanation of the code:-

1.   Use the function require to include the module events'. With this module, you can create events in node.js.
2.   Create a new transmitter of events. This is used to bind the event, which in our case is "data_received" to a callback function that is defined in step 3.

3.   We define a function which event said that if the event "data_received" is triggered, we must remove the text "data_received" to the console.

4.   Finally, we have a manual trigger of our event using the function eventEmiter.Emit. This will trigger the event data_received.

During the execution of the program, the text "Data received" will be sent to the console as shown below.

EMITTING EVENTS

During the definition of events, there are different methods for the events which can be invoked. This topic focuses on the detailed examination of each of them.

1.   Managers of single event

Sometimes, you may be interested to react to an event only the first time it occurs. In these situations, you can use the method once().

Let us see how we can use the method ounce for managers of events.

Code Explanation of the code:-

1.	Here, we use the method an ounce' to say that for the event'data_RECEIVED,' the callback function should be executed only once.

2.	Here, we throw manually the event'data_received'.

3.	When the event'data_received is again triggered, this time, nothing will happen. It is because of the first step where we have said that the event could not be triggered only once .

If the code is executed correctly, the output in the log will be'data_received successfully'. This message will only appear once in the console.

2.	Inspect the listeners of the event

Has any time of his life, a transmitter of events can have zero or more of listeners attached to the transmitter of events. The listeners for each type of event can be inspected in several ways.

If you are interested to determine only the number of listeners connected, look no further than the method EventEmitter.listenerCount().

(Note: the listeners are important because the main program should know if the listeners are added on the fly to an event, otherwise the emission operate poorly because of other auditors will be called.

Code Explanation of the code:-

1.   We are in the process of defining a type of eventEmitter which is necessary to use the event methods.

2.   Then we are in the process of defining an object called a transmitter which will be used to define our managers of events.

3.   We are in the process of creating 2 events managers who do nothing. This is simple for our example to show how does the method listenerCount.

4.   Now, when you invoke the method listenerCount on our data Event_received, it will send the number of event listeners attached to this event in the log of the console.

If the code is executed correctly, the value of 2 will be displayed in the console log.

3.   The event newListener

Each time a new event handler is registered, the transmitter of events emits a newListener event. This event is used to detect the new managers of events. You typically use the event newListener when you need to allocate resources or perform an action for each new event handler.

```
Var events = require( Events');
Var eventEmitter = events.EventEmitter;
Var emitter = new eventEmitter();
Emitter.On("newListener", function(EventName, listener) {
   Console.log("Added listener for " + eventName + "events");
});
Emitter.On('data_received', function() {});
```

```
Emitter.On('data_received', function() {});
```

Code Explanation of the code:-

1.   We are in the process of creating a new event handler for the event the newListener'. Thus, each time a new event handler is registered, the text "Added listener for" + the name of the event will be displayed in the console.

2.   Here, we write on the console the text "Added listener for" + the name of the event for each recorded event.

3.   We are in the process of defining 2 Managers of events for our event'data_received'.

If the above code is executed correctly, the text below will be displayed in the console. It simply shows that the manager of the events newListener' has been triggered twice.

Adding a listener for the events data_received.

Adding a listener for the events data_received.

Summary

- The use of the callback functions in node.js has its drawbacks. Sometimes, during the process of development, the use of nested callback functions can make the code more messy and difficult to maintain.

- Most of the problems with the functions of nested reminder can be mitigated by the use of promises and generators in node.js.

- A Promise is a value returned by a function asynchronous for indicate the completion of the processing performed by the asynchronous function.

- The promises can be nested within each other to make the code better and easier to maintain when many asynchronous functions must be called at the same time.

- The generators can also be used to alleviate the problems related to Reminders nested and help to eliminate what is called the hell of the reminder. The generators are used to stop the treatment of a function. This is accomplished by the use of the method to yield' in the asynchronous function.

- The flows are used in node.js for read and write the data of input devices-output. Node.js uses the Library The fs' to create flows readable and writable drives in the files. These flows can be used to read and write data from files.

- The pipes can be used to connect multiple streams together. One of the most common examples is to channel the flow of reading and writing for the transfer of data from a file to another.

- Node.js is also often labeled as a framework based on the events, and it is very easy to define events in node.js. It is possible to define functions that respond to these events.

- The events also exposes the methods of intervention in the case of key events. For example, we have seen the event handler ounce() which can be used to ensure that a callback function is executed only once when an event is triggered.

Chapter 8: test with jasmine

The test is a key element of any application. For node.js, the framework available for testing is called Jasmine. At the beginning of the year 2000, there was a framework for testing applications javascript JsUnit called. Later, this framework has been updated and is now known under the name of jasmine.

Jasmine helps to automate the unit tests, which has become a key practice during the development and deployment of modern Web applications.

In this tutorial, you will learn how to configure your environment with jasmine and how to begin to test your first application node.js with jasmine.

OVERVIEW OF JASMINE TO TEST THE APPLICATIONS NODE.JS

Jasmine is a test framework for JavaScript of Behavior Driven Development(BDD). It is not based on the browsers, the DOM or any other JavaScript framework. Thus, it is suitable for Web sites, to projects node.js, or to any other place where JavaScript can run. To begin to use Jasmine, you must first download and install the modules Jasmine needed.

Then, you will need to initialize your environment and inspect the configuration file of jasmine. The steps below show how to configure Jasmine in your environment.

Step 1) Installation of Modules NPM
To use the framework Jasmine from an application node, the jasmine module must first be installed. To install the module jasmine-node, run the command below.
Npm install jasmine-node

Step 2) Initialization of the project - in doing this, Jasmine creates a directory for specification and configuration JSON for you. The directory spec is used to store all your test files. In doing this, Jasmine will know where all your tests, and can then execute them accordingly. The JSON file is used to store configuration information specific to jasmine.
To initialize the environment Jasmin, run the command below
Jasmine init

Step 3) Inspect your configuration file. The configuration file will be stored in the folder spec/support under the name Jasmine.Json. This file lists the source files and the files of specifying that you want to include in the runner Jasmine.

The screenshot below shows a typical example of the package file.Json for Jasmine.

1.   Note that the directory of specifications is specified here. As indicated previously, when Jasmine runs, it search all tests in this directory.

2.   The next thing to note is the parameter spec_files - This indicates that the test files, what they may be, must be added with the keyword'spec'.

HOW TO USE JASMINE TO TEST THE APPLICATIONS NODE.JS?

In order to use Jasmine to test the Applications node.js, a series of steps must be followed.

In our example below, we will define a module that adds 2 numbers that must be tested. We will then define a separate code file with the test code and then use Jasmine to test the function add accordingly.

Step 1) define the code to test. We are going to define a function that will add 2 numbers and return the result. This code will be written to a file called "Add.js".

```
Var exports=module.exports={};
Exports.AddNumber=function(a,b)
{
Return a+b;
};
```

Code Explanation of the Code:

1.   The keyword "exports" is used to ensure that the functionality defined in this file is actually accessible by other files.

2.   We are in the process of defining a function called AddNumber The'. This function is defined to take 2 parameters, a and b. The function is added to the module "exports" to make the function a public service accessible by other modules of application.

3.   We are finally making of our function return the value added of the settings.

Step 2) then we must define our test code Jasmin which will be used to test our function "Add" in the file Add.js. The code below must be placed in a file called add-spec.js.

Note: - the word'spec' must be added to the test file so that it can be detected by jasmine.

```
Var app=require("../Add.js");
Describe("Addition",function(){
It("The function should add 2 numbers",function() {
Var value=app.AddNumber(5.6);
Expect(value).toBe(11);
});
```

```
});
```

Code Explanation:

1.   First we need to include our file Add.js in order to be able to test the function of AddNumber' in this file.

2.   We are in the process of creating our module to test. The first part of the test module is to describe a method which essentially gives a name to our test. In this case, the name of our test is "Addition".

3.   The next bit is to give a description of our test using the method it'.

4.   We shall now invoke our method Addnumber and send 2 parameters 5 and 6. This will be forwarded to our Addnumber method in the file App.JS. The return value is then stored in a variable called value.

5.   The final step is to make the comparison or our real test. Since we expect that the value returned by the function Addnumber either 11, we define this using the method expect(value).toBe(the expected value).

Exit

1.   To run the test, it must execute the command Jasmine.

2.   The screenshot below shows that after the execution of the command jasmine, it will detect that there is a test called add-spec.js and run this test accordingly. If there are errors in the test, it will be displayed accordingly.

Summary

•   In order to test an application node.js, The Framework jasmine must first be installed. This is done by using the package manager node.

•   The test code must be written in a separate file, and the word'spec' must be added to the name of the file. Only if this is fact that Jasmine will be able to detect that a file must be executed.

•   To run the test, you must execute the command Jasmine. This will find all files that have the word'spec' attached to the word 'spec' and will execute the file accordingly.

One last thing...

You liked the book?

If this is the case, please let me know by leaving a comment on Amazon! The criticisms are the soul of the authors independent. I would appreciate even a few words and an assessment if that is all you have the time to do so.

If you have not enjoyed this book, then tell me! EMAIL me and tell me what you have not liked! By phase, I can change. In the world of today, a book does not need to be stagnant, it may improve with time and the comments from readers like you. You can have an impact on this book, and I invite you to share your comments with me. Help us to improve this book for all the world!